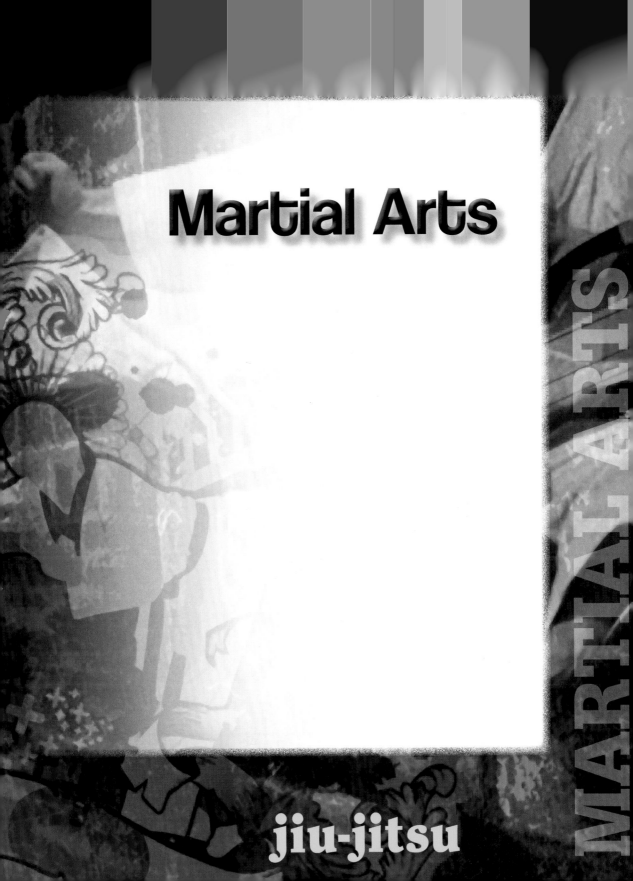

Martial Arts

jiu-jitsu

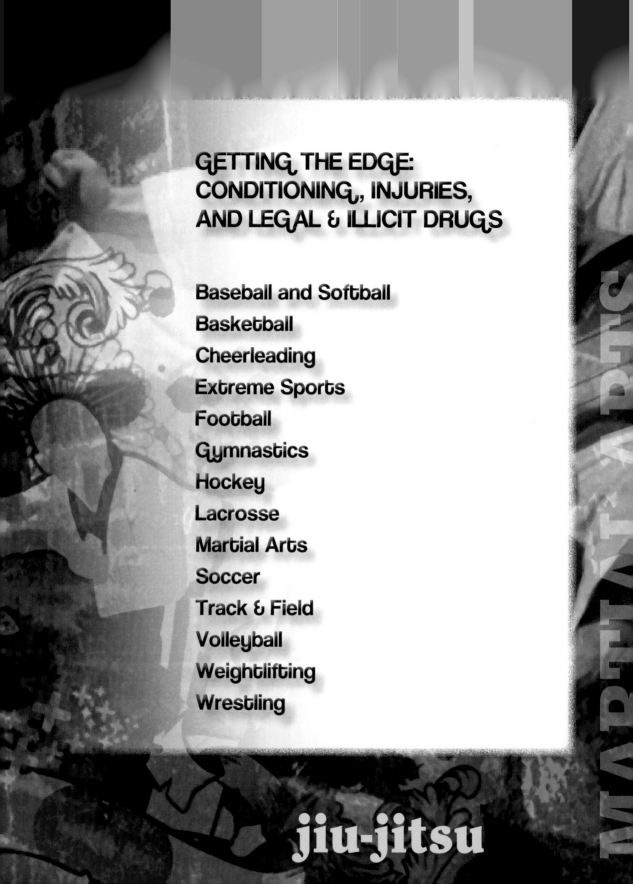

GETTING THE EDGE: CONDITIONING, INJURIES, AND LEGAL & ILLICIT DRUGS

Baseball and Softball

Basketball

Cheerleading

Extreme Sports

Football

Gymnastics

Hockey

Lacrosse

Martial Arts

Soccer

Track & Field

Volleyball

Weightlifting

Wrestling

MARTIAL ARTS

jiu-jitsu

Martial Arts

by J. S. McIntosh

Mason Crest Publishers

jiu-jitsu

MASON CREST PUBLISHERS INC.
370 Reed Road
Broomall, Pennsylvania 19008
(866)MCP-BOOK (toll free)
www.masoncrest.com

First Printing
9 8 7 6 5 4 3 2 1

Library of Congress Cataloging-in-Publication Data

McIntosh, J. S.
  Martial arts / by J.S. McIntosh.
      p. cm. — (Getting the edge : conditioning, injuries, and legal & illicit drugs)
  Includes bibliographical references and index.
  ISBN 978-1-4222-1738-2   ISBN (series) 978-1-4222-1728-3
  1. Martial arts—Juvenile literature. 2. Martial arts—Training. I. Title.
  GV1101.35.M36 2011
  796.8—dc22
                              2010012753

Produced by Harding House Publishing Service, Inc.
www.hardinghousepages.com
Interior Design by MK Bassett-Harvey.
Cover Design by Torque Advertising + Design.
Printed in the USA by Bang Printing.

The creators of this book have made every effort to provide accurate information, but it should not be used as a substitute for the help and services of trained professionals.

Contents

karate, jiu-jitsu, judo

Introduction

GETTING THE EDGE: CONDITIONING, INJURIES, AND LEGAL & ILLICIT DRUGS is a fourteen-volume series written for young people who are interested in learning about various sports and how to participate in them safely. Each volume examines the history of the sport and the rules of play; it also acts as a guide for prevention and treatment of injuries, and includes instruction on stretching, warming up, and strength training, all of which can help players avoid the most common musculoskeletal injuries. Each volume also includes tips on healthy nutrition for athletes, as well as information on the risks of using performance-enhancing drugs or other illegal substances. GETTING THE EDGE offers ways for readers to healthily and legally improve their performance and gain more enjoyment from playing sports. Young athletes will find these volumes informative and helpful in their pursuit of excellence.

Sports medicine professionals assigned to a sport with which they are not familiar can also benefit from this series. For example, a football athletic trainer may need to provide medical care for a local gymnastics meet. Although the emergency medical principles and action plan would remain the same, the athletic trainer could provide better care for the gymnasts after reading a simple overview of the principles of gymnastics in GETTING THE EDGE.

Although these books offer an overview, they are not intended to be comprehensive in the recognition and management of sports injuries. They should not replace the professional advice of a trainer, doctor, or nutritionist. The text helps the reader appreciate and gain awareness of the sport's history, standard training techniques, common injuries, dietary guidelines,

karate, jiu-jitsu, judo

and the dangers of using drugs to gain an advantage. Reference material and directed readings are provided for those who want to delve further into these subjects.

Written in a direct and easily accessible style, GETTING THE EDGE is an enjoyable series that will help young people learn about sports and sports medicine.

—*Susan Saliba, Ph.D., National Athletic Trainers' Association Education Council*

MARTIAL ARTS

1
Overview of Martial Arts

Understanding the Words

A **low-impact** *activity is one that does not involve your body parts (usually your feet) striking against a hard surface.*

Bonobos *are a kind of tree-dwelling ape that are more slender and with longer limbs than chimpanzees.*

A **prodigy** *is a young person with extraordinary talents or intelligence for his or her age.*

Something that is **obscure** *is hidden, not obvious or well-known.*

jiu-jitsu

karate, jiu-jitsu, judo

And those brave tigers among men then cheerfully engaged in a wrestling combat, desirous of vanquishing each other. And terrible was the encounter that took place between them, like the clash of the thunderbolt against the stony mountain-breast. And both of them were exceedingly powerful and extremely delighted at each other's strength.
—The Mahabharata

Martial arts—systems of movement in which a practitioner defends himself or herself through force—have been around a long time. The quotation above was written between 4 and 6 thousand years ago!

In many ways, martial arts are unlike any other sport. They can be classified as belonging both to athletic sports and to the arts, for example, and they have a practical application for self-defense. Martial arts also almost always have long-standing (if not ancient) traditions, and some are linked to religious or spiritual practices.

Hundreds of different martial arts are currently practiced. Some martial arts feature competitions in the form of sparring (staged, controlled fights). Other martial arts compete by performing dance-like maneuvers. Some martial arts involve deflecting your opponent's energy against them; in others, the practitioner strikes his enemy. With so many variations, pinning all martial arts down to a single definition becomes difficult! Perhaps an easier question to answer is this: how are martial arts practiced?

Martial arts are practiced using defined movements such as arm or leg strikes, grappling moves, throws, or the use of weapons. There are also

DID YOU KNOW?

Martial arts aren't only practiced in Asia; well-defined systems of self-defense are found throughout every corner of the globe. Europe, the Americas, and Africa all have their own traditions. New martial arts have risen from different cultures combining or clashing. All martial arts practiced now are the result of many traditions mixing together.

MARTIAL ARTS

karate, jiu-jitsu, judo

low-impact martial arts like tai chi, which involve meditative movements performed gently and slowly.

Martial Arts: Many Histories

PRE-HUMAN ORIGINS TO ANCIENT HISTORY

Martial arts have been around as long as the human race has recorded events. In fact, one could argue that organized fighting without the intent of physical harm goes back before humans. Chimpanzees and **bonobos** wrestle among siblings and between parents and children, and many scientists believe that these primates are the closest evolutionary link to humans. The primates apparently play-fight among each other to reduce tension and educate their young.

Humans have practiced martial arts for thousands of years. Some scientists think that fighting without trying to harm pre-dates modern humans.

MARTIAL ARTS

karate, jiu-jitsu, judo

When it comes to humans, though, many historians believe that Asian martial arts originated in India and moved to China during the spread of Buddhism in the first centuries of the Common Era. The fact that Chinese and Indian martial arts share many similarities supports this theory. Other historians think that the two traditions could have developed in the same direction without any direct contact between the two. In any case, martial arts traveled from China to other regions further east, such as Japan and Korea. In Japan, Chinese martial arts developed into karate. In Korea they developed into tae kwan-do. Today, these two forms of martial arts are the most popular in the United States.

KARATE

Karate originated in the Ryukyu Kingdom in the nineteenth century. Chinese martial arts—called "Kempo" once they reached Japan—migrated to a small group of islands near the south of mainland Japan. From there, karate spread to other parts of Japan in the early 1900s during a period of cultural sharing with smaller neighboring islands.

In 1922, a karate master gave a demonstration in Tokyo, and by 1932, all Japanese universities had their own dojo, or training center. Before Japan invaded China during World War II, karate's name changed from being known as the "Chinese hand" to "empty hand."

In the 1960s and 1970s, martial arts movies made karate increasingly popular and the sport grew popular in the rest of the world, especially in America. Today, hundreds of thousands of athletes practice karate around the world.

TAE KWON DO

Understanding the early history of Korean martial arts is difficult, because from 1910 to 1945, Japan occupied Korea and tried to replace Korean culture with Japanese customs. As a result, scholars of the martial arts are uncertain

karate, jiu-jitsu, judo

Karate is a Japanese form of martial arts adapted from Chinese martial arts in the early 19th century.

Judo is another name for a form of jiu-jitsu (itself a Japanese form of wrestling) created by Kano Jigoro, the founder of many modern styles of wrestling, and updated in Brazil by Mitsuyo Maeda, a trainee of Jigoro.

karate, jiu-jitsu, judo

as to how much influence ancient Korean martial arts have on modern tae kwon do compared to the influence of karate.

After the Allied forces defeated Japan in World War II, Korea was free, and Korean martial arts schools opened up around the country. Nine major schools of martial arts were practiced around the country by the 1950s. In 1952, the president of South Korea, after watching a demonstration of a man breaking thirteen roof tiles with a punch, ordered that the army to be taught tae kwon do. At the same time, he unified all the martial arts being taught in Korea into one system. This was the birth of the organized form of tae kwon do. The South-Korean government approved the name tae kwon do on April 11, 1955. In the year 2000 tae kwon do became an Olympic sport in the year 2000.

BRAZILIAN JIU-JITSU (JUDO)

Brazilian jiu-jitsu has travelled from the islands of Japan to Brazil and the United States. The founder of modern wrestling arts, Kano Jigoro, invented the practice of "randori," which is controlled sparring with few rules—known as judo, which is simply updated jiu-jitsu. The two terms are sometimes interchangeable and both refer to Asian wrestling arts.

Mitsuyo Maeda was a student of Kano Jigoro, a prodigy with immense natural talent. Maeda won hundreds of matches, fighting in Europe and the United States, and then moved to Brazil, where he established a jiu-jitsu

academy. There in Brazil, Maeda updated judo to be more applicable to real-life self-defense. At the same time, he pushed judo toward becoming a competitive sport.

A particularly gifted student of Maeda, Carlos Gracie, moved to the United States from Brazil, winning many mixed martial arts matches in the 1990s. Gracie made Brazilian jiu-jitsu more popular through his victories.

Types of Martial Arts

Many different martial arts are practiced in the United States and around the world. They range from low-impact martial arts such as tae chi to holds and grabs in sports like jiu-jitso and judo to karate and tae kwon do, which are both based on strikes. These are the martial arts that are practiced most often in the United States. The full number of practiced martial arts is unknown, and new martial arts are often developed that are not regulated by any one organization. For instance, Bruce Lee created his own martial art called jeet kune do forty years ago and it is still practiced. The list of **obscure** martial arts that only a few people know is even larger. The list ranges from acudo (which is based on acupuncture points) to zipota (an old martial art from Spain).

Self-Defense

Self-defense is the most useful skill you can learn from a martial art. Karate originated in Japan because unarmed people needed to defend themselves. People that live in violent areas, especially women (who are often more vulnerable to violence) find karate useful not as a sport but simply as a practical way to protect themselves.

> **DID YOU KNOW?**
> Statistics show that a woman who fights back has an 86% higher chance of avoiding rape if attacked.

karate, jiu-jitsu, judo

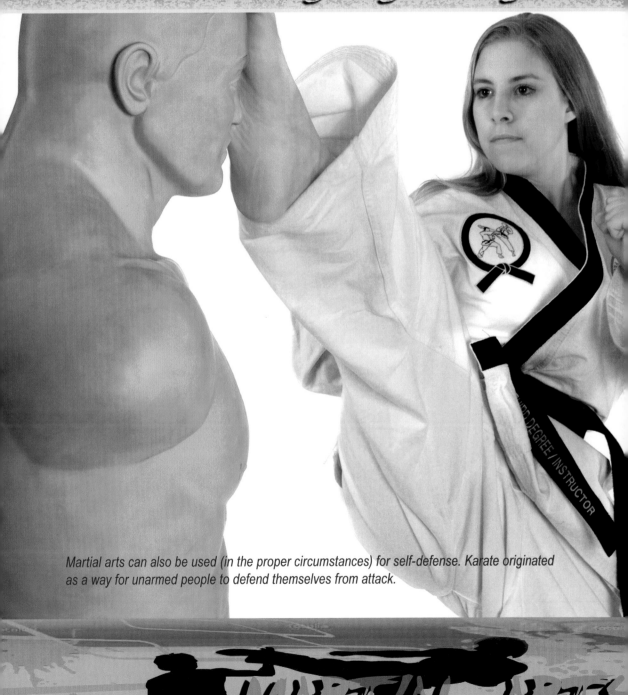

Martial arts can also be used (in the proper circumstances) for self-defense. Karate originated as a way for unarmed people to defend themselves from attack.

karate, jiu-jitsu, judo

Wise Words

While martial arts schools advertise that they teach "self-defense," this does not mean passively waiting to get into a situation where you are physically in danger. The greatest thing anyone can do to avoid a fight is to actively avoid dangerous situations. Crossing the road at the right time when a shady character is walking toward you on the street, asking a friend to accompany you while you walk in a bad neighborhood, carrying a rape-whistle, and always having your cell phone on you: all of these actions do much more for your safety than learning a new kick.

An anonymous quote on a dojo wall states, "Martial arts are not about being defensive. Being defensive is a terrible way to go through life." This quote does not mean a karate student should go out and start fights in the

Martial Arts Celebrity

Bruce Lee was born November 27, 1940, in San Francisco, California, but he grew up in Hong Kong. There he trained under a master in the martial art called wing chun. Many in China at the time did not believe that Chinese citizens who had mixed heritage should be taught martial arts. Bruce Lee's mother had German ancestors, but despite the social conventions, Yip Man, a famous Wing Chun master, began teaching Bruce Lee at age thirteen. After many successful tournaments, Bruce Lee went on to star in action films in the 1970s, and he made martial arts films famous in the United States. Bruce Lee also created his own martial art, jeet kune do, which is still practiced today.

karate, jiu-jitsu, judo

street but rather that we need to be proactive about life and our safety. Just because martial arts are called self-defense does not mean that students should wait until physical confrontation to defend themselves.

Careers in the Martial Arts

The majority of martial arts students do not turn their interest into a full-time career. Teaching a martial art is the main career path offered in martial arts. To operate a dojo, an instructor needs to have a passion for the martial art

The main career path for students of karate or other martial arts is to become a teacher of the martial art they have learned.

karate, jiu-jitsu, judo

What Are Mixed Martial Arts?

Mixed martial arts (MMA) is a combat sport that encompasses a combination of techniques from wrestling, boxing, kickboxing, karate, jiu-jitsu, judo, and muay thai, as well as many other striking and grappling styles. It is a full-contact combat sport that allows a wide variety of fighting techniques and skills to be used in competitions. Such competitions allow martial artists of different backgrounds to compete.

The roots of mixed martial arts can be traced back to various mixed-style contests that took place throughout Europe, Japan, and the Pacific Rim during the early 1900s, but modern MMA competition emerged in 1993 with the founding of the Ultimate Fighting Championship. Originally organized with the intention of finding the most effective martial arts for real unarmed combat situations, competitors were pitted against one another with minimal rules for safety. Later promoters adopted many additional rules aimed at increasing safety for competitors and to promote mainstream acceptance of the sport. The sport has become increasingly popular, with pay-per-view sales that rival boxing and professional wrestling.

and for teaching others. An instructor needs to have more skills than just knowing a martial art, however. She will also need to be able to monitor

karate, jiu-jitsu, judo

her students' classes and maintain safety and discipline (especially if they include children or young adults), be a good teacher, know how to advertise her classes, and sometimes be able to give lectures to the community, educating others about the martial art. Continued education is also important. In martial arts, everyone is always a student.

Some exceptional athletes are able to compete for a living. Mixed martial arts are currently popular. Knowing a martial art can also be helpful for careers in law enforcement and the military, but it is not required.

A Way of Life

The Japanese word "do" is a translation of the Chinese term tao, which means "way of life." Many karate teachers call their martial art karate-do to emphasize that karate is more than a tool to defend oneself; it's a way of living. Notice that "do" is also at the end of "tae kwan do" and other martial arts' names, such as "kendo," "akido," "judo." The word "dojo" (the word for a martial arts center for training) means literally "a place where the Way is taught." Keep in mind that all martial arts are more than a way to defend yourself. They are also far more than a sport or an exercise. Martial arts teach ways of living in harmony with yourself and with others.

2
Balanced Mind, Safe Body: Mental Preparation

Understanding the Words

Preoccupy *means to absorb the thoughts, to distract the thoughts, or to excessively concern the mind.*

Detach *means to separate from.*

Someone who is **conservative** *prefers to stick with traditional ideas and ways of doing things and is less open to new ideas.*

Adherence *is the faithful practice of or devotion to a way of doing something.*

jiu-jitsu

MARTIAL ARTS

Wise Words: Yoda

Yoda, perhaps the most famous martial arts sensei in all of cinema, has wise words to say about the need to control the mind. In the movie **Star Wars**, the 800-year-old master trains Luke Skywalker in the ways of Jedi. Yoda tells Luke to control his emotions: "Fear leads to anger. Anger leads to hate. Hate leads to suffering." While Yoda may not be real, this saying has value.

There is a famous karate saying: *Shingi ittai*, which means, "Mind and technique are one." This is important to all martial arts. From the performance of a *Kata* (a set of performed movements) to a sparring match to actual self-defense on the street, in martial arts we need our mind to be in-sync with our techniques. Often the mind will affect the body (just as the body can affect the mind).

Randall Hassell, a chief instructor for the American Shotokan Karate Alliance and writer on karate topics, describes an important point his *sensei* (teacher) made about the link between body and mind. When his instructor told him to stretch out his body completely, Randall confessed that he could never fully stretch his body; he said his body was too stiff. His sensei replied with a smile, "No, your mind is too stiff. Stiff mind, stiff body. Release mind; body will follow."

This is a crucial point in mental preparedness in karate. Martial artists, especially beginners, need to make sure to always have an open, clear mind when they stretch, when they practice, and when they engage in competition. By doing this, they ensure their technique is perfectly aligned with an open mind.

MARTIAL ARTS

In martial arts, control over your mind and emotions is just as important as control over your body and actions.

Self-Control

There is a phrase heard often in tae kwon do—"watch your control"—that underlines the need to put the body under the mind's control. One of the benefits of a martial art is that it teaches you the discipline to control your body in all situations. When you strike someone in tae kwon do, for example, you are not throwing a punch at your opponent; you are placing a carefully aimed strike.

Ask yourself during practice: are you in control? If there isn't a resounding, "yes," then you are practicing sloppily and incorrectly, and you are not

karate, jiu-jitsu, judo

practicing safely. A strike that is well placed benefits both you and your sparring partner: it protects him from the risk of injury, and it helps you win. A kick that is accurate is more likely to win a match.

Controlling your emotions is crucial as well. You need a mind that is clear from anger. An attacker with an angry mind is likely to lose to lose a fight to a defender with an open, alert mind. Anger clouds the thinking, which leads to not only bad fighting but even worse, bad judgment. If you use violence when it is not absolutely necessary, you can end up with a lawsuit, an arrest, or an injury—or even a death. Martial arts students learn self-control in their dojos, and they make sure they "watch their control," never throwing punches but rather carefully placing them.

Concentration: Empty Mind

To fully practice a martial art you must achieve the state of an empty

Anger diminishes clear thinking and makes winning martial arts matches more difficult, not less. Relieving your mind of negative thoughts is a far better path to victory than fighting in anger.

karate, jiu-jitsu, judo

Wise Words: The Journey Itself

In the United States, we place great importance on achievements and setting goals. While these things are important, we must remember that in martial arts there is always more to learn; students never reach a point of complete mastery. Instead, martial arts require constant learning and relearning of techniques and movements. Think of it like a journey that never ends. As the Japanese poet Matsuo Basho said in a haiku, "each day is a journey, and the journey itself is home."

mind. This should not to be confused with absent-minded carelessness. You want to be focused and mindful of what you are doing. The empty-mindedness necessary for martial arts asks that you let go of all the things that normally preoccupy you. As you walk into the dojo, try to leave at the door your worries—the fight you had with a friend, the homework that's due tomorrow, the concert you're hoping your parents will let you attend—as well as the things that are making you happy—the good grade you got on your math exam, the big date coming up on the weekend, the after-school job you just landed. Detach your thoughts from whatever distracts you from the present moment. At the most basic level, you should only be thinking about your body and your breathing.

An empty mind is a mind that occupies only the present. As a result, an empty mind will act quickly and strike more accurately. When you free your mind from problems and distractions, you will be able to immediately and freely move your attention wherever it needs to go. If you think of your mind

as an engine, the less that gets in the way of the engine running, the faster the engine can accelerate.

A free mind focused only on the present moment gives the martial arts student the ability to perform movements without conscious thought. Self-defense will occur automatically. The point of training and practice is not to provide a series of movements to memorize but rather to build automatic reflexes. When the moment arises, you shouldn't have to think to yourself, "Should I perform a roundhouse kick or a punch?" Instead, the movement should flow without effort. By fully emptying the mind and concentrating, you allow your muscles and subconscious thoughts to do the work for you.

MEDITATION: A TOOL FOR EMPTYING YOUR MIND

Meditation is an important tool in clearing your mind before practice at a dojo or in a competition. When we meditate, we don't technically "do" anything. Instead, we try to undo our normal thought process. Meditation is the conscious effort to clear the mind.

When you meditate you should be in a comfortable position (but not too comfortable: sleep isn't meditation!), sitting upright. Concentrate the mind on nothing but your breathing. Anyone who tries to meditate for the first time will tell you that it doesn't take long to encounter difficulty. Our minds are in the habit of wandering from one thought to the next as we perform each day's task. It takes effort and practice to retrain our minds and build new habits.

Meditation helps performance in martial arts. When you meditate, you clear the mind, freeing yourself from all the other elements of your life that distract your attention. This state of mind then extends into the active portion of your time in the dojo.

When you practice martial arts, you aren't only practicing self-defense; you are also engaging in exercises in thinking in the present moment. When you

karate, jiu-jitsu, judo

Meditation helps to clear the mind so that martial artists may focus on their performance, rather than potential distractions.

MARTIAL ARTS

karate, jiu-jitsu, judo

are sparring with someone, the clearer your perception, the more successful you will be. Meditation is an important starting point for achieving a mind that is focused on the here-and-now.

Martial artists can take more from martial arts than exercise or entertainment. In many ways, martial arts are as much about the mind as they are the body.

karate, jiu-jitsu, judo

Religion and Martial Arts

According to the Christian Research Foundation, of all martial arts, tae kwon do has been influenced least by Eastern religions. Martial arts such as tai chi and kung fu are based on a combination of Chinese Taoism and Confucianism. Japanese martial arts such as karate are based on Zen Buddhism, which places importance on emptiness and being present-minded.

Spirituality: Eastern Religion in a Western Dojo

Many ideas in Asian martial arts about the body and mind are based on Eastern religion and philosophy. Martial arts moved east to Asia from India during the spread of Buddhism, and as a result, karate has roots in Buddhism.

Some conservative Western Christians have opposed martial arts, saying that they are in conflict with the teachings of Christianity. However, many martial arts students are practicing Christians. Sensei Thomas Shea, for example, writes that he does not see any conflict between karate and the teachings of Jesus.

Others see martial arts as simply a sport or a form of exercise; they do not feel that a total understanding of (let alone adherence to) the spiritual philosophies at the foundation of a particular martial art is necessary to enjoying and benefiting from that martial art's athleticism and discipline.

karate, jiu-jitsu, judo

For many young adults, martial arts are a great way to make friends, get exercise, and learn something new. For others, martial arts can be a way of life.

karate, jiu-jitsu, judo

Wise Words from Bruce Lee

"Effort within the mind further limits the mind, because effort implies struggle towards a goal and when you have a goal, a purpose, an end in view, you have placed a limit on the mind."

—Bruce Lee

Some martial arts are more spiritual in nature than others. However, while some knowledge of Eastern philosophy is necessary at deeper levels of study, martial arts dojos do not force their students to convert to any religion or to give up their own faith!

Mind and Body

As important as mental attitudes are to the martial arts, all martial arts teach that both the mind and the body must be developed together. Training should be split evenly between the two to achieve the balance that is so vital to the martial arts.

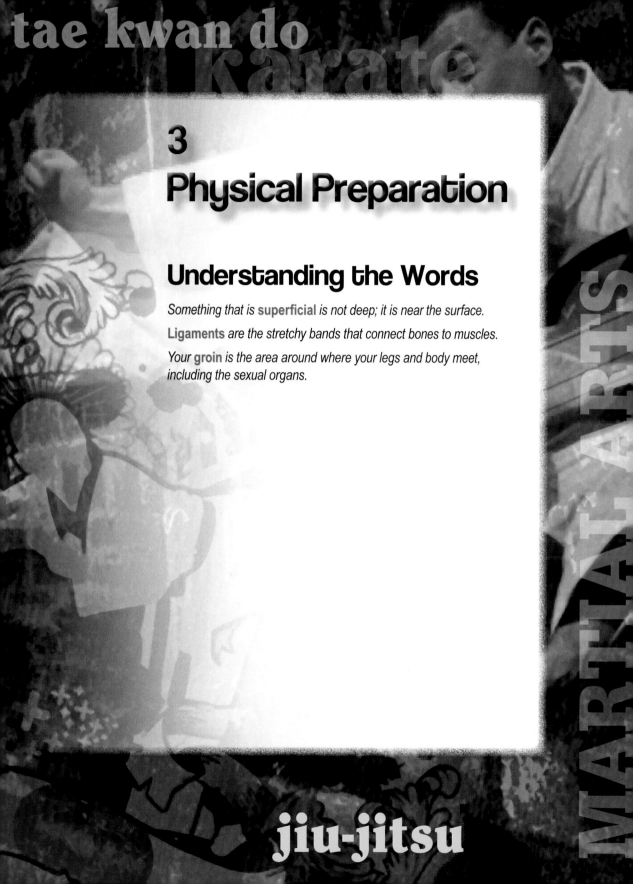

3
Physical Preparation

Understanding the Words

*Something that is **superficial** is not deep; it is near the surface.*

***Ligaments** are the stretchy bands that connect bones to muscles.*

*Your **groin** is the area around where your legs and body meet, including the sexual organs.*

karate, jiu-jitsu, judo

As martial arts students prepare themselves physically, they will also be protecting both the safety of their own bodies and the safety of their opponents as well. Injury prevention is a two-way street in the martial arts. We need to prevent injuries to ourselves and also prevent ourselves from injuring others. All students of martial arts need to practice these safety techniques.

Keep it Flexible: The Importance of Stretching

Stretching before training or competing is crucial for martial arts students. It's one of the easiest ways to prevent injuries. A good stretch warms up the muscles so that they do not tear when extended. Stretches should be done before practice begins, usually after a warm-up such as a light jog.

Too often, however, an injury occurs even after **superficial** stretches have been done, because the major muscles have been stretched but not the smaller muscles and **ligaments**. These small muscles are important, especially when asking your legs to endure the strain of a sudden, extreme move like a high kick.

STRETCHING EXERCISES

The specific martial art you practice may call for more stretches in one part of the body than another. In karate, for instance, the arms will be important, in tae kwon do, flexible legs need to be thoroughly stretched. Because martial arts differ dramatically and because different parts of the body need to be stretched for each discipline, consult your instructor for a particular stretching regimen (schedule and method of exercise). What follows here is a list of stretches that will be helpful for any martial art.

karate, jiu-jitsu, judo

Stretching before practice or a match is the best way to prevent injury. Holding stretches for around a minute is usually most effective in warming up muscles before athletic activity.

karate, jiu-jitsu, judo

Wise Words from Gichin Funakoshi

Gichin Funakoshi, who was born in 1870 in Okinawa, brought karate from Okinawa to the larger islands of Japan. After he showed his skills in Tokyo in 1922, karate grew to such popularity that he stayed in Tokyo to teach. Stories circulated of masters breaking stones with their hands, but Funakoshi was skeptical of far-fetched stories of karate feats. What's more, he did not think this was the real point of practicing karate. He stated,

> **"Those who take pride in breaking boards or smashing tiles . . . really know nothing about karate. They are playing around in the leaves and branches of a great tree, without the slightest concept of the trunk."**

Hamstring

While lying on the floor, put one foot toward the ceiling and hold while the other leg is straight on the ground. Alternate legs and repeat. You should feel stress on the back of your thigh.

Thighs

Put legs in a V shape while sitting. Repeatedly lean the chest forward, keeping it straight.

karate, jiu-jitsu, judo

Hips

While lying on your back, pull both knees to your chest and wrap your arms around them. While your right knee stays bent, bring the left leg onto the floor. Drop the right knee gently to the left. Turn your head toward the opposite direction. Repeat, alternating sides.

Shoulders

While in a squatting position, put your hands on your knees. Rotate right shoulder toward the floor. Alternate shoulders. Extend feet shoulder-length apart, while they face the same direction. Roll the shoulders backward, then forward.

This stretch will help loosen your thighs. The more often you stretch, the more flexible you will become.

MARTIAL ARTS

karate, jiu-jitsu, judo

More Wise Words from Bruce Lee

Bruce Lee held a great interest in performing martial arts movements as efficiently as possible. He stated: "I fear not the man who has practiced 10,000 kicks once, but I fear the man who has practiced one kick 10,000 times." In other words: don't worry about the quantity (or number) of techniques you learn. The main benefit you get from training is to form quality in your physical movements. The best way to do this is through repetition of the same movements. Practice. Practice. Practice.

Biceps

Sit cross-legged. Place palms onto the floor, and face your thumbs toward the back of the room. Try to place your whole palm on the floor.

Back

Place feet parallel to each other, shoulder-length apart. Place hands around your back. Bend forward.

Neck

Lean your head toward the left shoulder, then your right shoulder. Lower your head toward the ground and then the ceiling. Rotate your neck by turning your head all the way left, then right.

Waist

While feet are hip-width apart, face forward. Then, while exhaling through the mouth, bend forward slowly. Continue until your arms are stretched toward the ground. Take deep breaths. Slowly rise back up, as if unrolling your spine.

karate, jiu-jitsu, judo

The martial arts student learns many skills in the dojo, both mental and physical.

MARTIAL ARTS

karate, jiu-jitsu, judo

Training and Conditioning

One difference between martial arts and other sports is that in American sports, the athletes train for the sake of competing, focusing their mind on a basketball match or football game. While competition is a major part of training in martial arts, it is not the central focus. Instead the purpose of martial arts is to improving one's entire way of life through self-defense training. Different martial arts schools and styles have different ways of achieving the goal of self-improvement.

BASIC TRAINING

This is called *kihon* in karate, where beginners are first introduced to basic movements, while masters hone movements they have practiced many times before.

FORMS

Forms are a series of controlled movements involving punches, kicks, blocks, and any other movement. In karate, these are known as *kata*; in tae kwon do, they are known as *poomse*. They assist the martial arts pupil in knowing how to apply basic movements and improve balance and concentration.

SPARRING

Sparring is the application of self-defense with a partner in a controlled setting. The martial arts practitioner will apply the same movements she learned in basic training against a live person.

SELF-DEFENSE EXERCISES

In a dojo, a student will learn ways to get out of grips and holds by learning throws, blocks, and various strikes. These self-defense exercises are real-life applications based on knowledge gained from other training.

karate, jiu-jitsu, judo

BREAKING

In some martial arts centers, students will focus their energy and strength against a physical object like a board or brick. Breaking objects can be part of testing to get to a higher belt-level.

Martial artists will often spar with a partner in order to practice the techniques they have learned.

MARTIAL ARTS

karate, jiu-jitsu, judo

Wise Words: Gichin Funakoshi

Gichin Funakoshi stated that the point of training is not to simply go through the motions but to find the essence of karate. He once said:

> **"You may train for a long time, but if you merely move your hands and feet and jump up and down like a puppet, learning karate is not very different from learning a dance. You will never have reached the heart of the matter; you will have failed to grasp the quintessence of karate-do."**

Protecting the Body: Staying Safe

While martial arts train their students to defend themselves against injuries, students also need to guard against injuring themselves in the dojo. Here are some safety suggestions that are true for all martial arts:

- There are hundreds of martial arts from which to choose. If you are not sure which martial art would be best for you, observe some different martial arts classes. While watching a class, you can evaluate how physically demanding that dojo will be.

- Obey your sensei. If he sets boundaries for you, there is a good reason.

- If you do not feel in control of your own movements, ask advice from your sensei or evaluate if the martial art is right for you.

karate, jiu-jitsu, judo

- Wear appropriate equipment (see later on in the chapter for more details).

- Put an emphasis on fun. A martial arts student should not feel stressed or pressured to achieve. The more relaxed you are, the more safe and more effective you will be.

- Make sure your peripheral vision is working. The better your coordination, the less likely you will receive a blow. If you think your vision isn't working at 100 percent, consult an optometrist.

LIGHT, MEDIUM, AND FULL-CONTACT MARTIAL ARTS

Sparring matches differ in intensity. Some schools do not allow any hitting; other schools have only light hits to the body where students "pull" their punches. This light-contact sparring means that competitors do not fully hit the other person and quickly pull back when contact is made. In medium-impact sparring, the punches are not pulled, but strikes are still not made with full force. Both light- and medium-contact sparring limits which parts of the body may be struck. Usually, strikes to the groin area are prohibited, and strikes to the face are either limited or not allowed. Medium-contact and light-contact matches are decided by a point system. The competitor that gets in the highest amount of strikes gets more points and wins the match.

In full-contact sparring, also called fighting, punches are not pulled; they are delivered with full force. In most full-contact matches the aim of the match is either to knock out the opponent or to force him to submit (give up the match). Some martial arts matches (such as tae kwon do) are full contact but are based on a system of points. Most mixed martial arts are full contact. Some martial arts do not involve actual strikes but are full contact because

karate jiu–jitsu judo

MARTIAL ARTS

karate, jiu-jitsu, judo

there are fewer restrictions on how contestants can attack their opponent. In Brazilian ju-jitsu and judo matches, submission techniques are executed with full force.

SPARRING EQUIPMENT

Martial arts differ in the safety equipment they require. Children use more equipment than adults (and children do not make direct hits to each other). The AAU National Karate Program requires that adult competitors (age nineteen and older) wear fist pads, a mouth guard, and a groin protector (for men). The organization requires that children wear also white foam headgear with a chinstrap. In tae kwon do, officials require that contestants wear a head and mouth guard, a hogu (body protector), groin guard, and forearm and shin guards. Competitors cannot wear glasses or jewelry during matches. For wrestling sports like jiu-jitsu and judo, headgear is required for all divisions under the age of sixteen, but headgear is not required for adults; gloves and shoes can only be half an inch thick; competitors cannot wear equipment or clothing that is too rough, torn, or loose; and contestants cannot wear hard plastic or metal equipment.

REFEREES

Martial arts organizations that hold matches always use referees. A referee regulates the match and watches for illegal moves. A separate panel of judges keeps track of points between matches.

The AAU National Karate Program requires adults to wear protective pads while competing, including headgear, body pads, and mouth guards. Men are required to wear groin protectors as well.

karate, jiu-jitsu, judo

Dojo

To begin in a martial art the student must first find a dojo. A dojo is a place of learning; it is called a dojang in tae kwon do and kwoon in Chinese martial arts like kung fu.

It is important to find a good fit for you. Not all places of learning are the same and instructors vary. Keep these factors into account when looking for a dojo:

- **Price**. Dojos will vary in price and some have fees to test for another belt. Also, find out how much competition will cost. In other words, make sure there are not many extra fees attached to attending the school.
- **Schedule**. Dojos vary in the availability of classes. At some, you can attend as many as you want each week. Other instructors are limited and offer fewer classes a week at scheduled times. Also, some dojos offer private

karate, jiu-jitsu, judo

lessons but not all do. Find out what works with your schedule.

- **Students**. Find out about the other students. This is important because if you train at this dojo, these people will be training alongside you and perhaps sparring with you. Make sure the dojo has a screening process. Also, find out if children will train with adults. Classes that are only filled with adults will move at a faster pace.
- **Teacher**. Next to safety issues, this is the most important factor. The sensei will set the tone for training and instruct you. Make sure you find a good fit. Do an Internet search and make sure all teachers at the dojo are certified through their school of martial arts. Make sure the sensei is professional and committed to teaching students.

4

Common Injuries, Treatment, & Recovery

Understanding the Words

Stances *are standing postures; positions in which a person stands.*

Fractures *are breaks (as in broken bones).*

Acute *means sharp, very serious.*

Thrombosis *is a blood clot inside a blood vessel.*

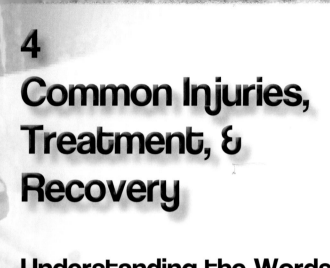

jiu-jitsu

MARTIAL ARTS

karate, jiu-jitsu, judo

Some kinds of injury are more common in one martial art than in another. For instance, in karate, practitioners are more likely to suffer from hand injuries, but judo students are more prone to joint dislocations. The martial arts also differ in the risk of injury involved. Among popular martial arts, tae kwon do is the most dangerous. The main reason is that in tae kwon do, higher points are earned for kicks to the head. This encourages competitors to spar more dangerously.

Light Injuries

The largest number of martial arts injuries fall into this category. Through receiving blows and blocking them, minor bruising and small cuts can occur. Bloody noses can happen if the face is struck in karate or tae kwon do. In jiu-jitsu and

DID YOU KNOW?
Tae kwon do injuries are three times as likely to occur as karate injuries.

You Are in Control

The dojo you attend is an important factor in your chance of being injured. Ask yourself: Is your dojo safe? Do you feel comfortable sparring with other members of the dojo? Does your sensei stress the importance of self-control? If there is any doubt that the answer is "yes" to any of these questions, find another place to study martial arts.

The most important safety factor cannot be calculated—because it's you! By controlling your movements, being mindful, staying calm, and being aware of your body's limitations, you won't be another injury statistic.

karate, jiu-jitsu, judo

Pushing Hands

Tai chi, the most gentle of martial arts, has its own sparring system, which is the lowest impact way to compete. There are no punches or kicks; instead, the participant pushes her partner off balance. By moving their hands in circular motions, the participants try to control the each other's energy. Shoving or sudden movements are prohibited. The tai chi practitioner who can push the other participant out of balance wins the match. Pushing hands is an option for a martial arts practitioner that is at high risk for injury.

judo, bloody lips sometimes result from being rubbed hard against a part of the wrestling partner's elbow or arm. Usually, wearing a mouthguard will protect against this.

There is some risk in overextending the ligaments, causing a sprain. (A sprain occurs when the connection between the joints is torn.) This commonly occurs in the leg ligaments as well as the spine. Many bent-knee **stances** and forceful kicks can cause injury to the knee joints.

Moderate Injuries

Fractures, dislocations, and damage to the nerves are a risk in martial arts that put an emphasis on fast movements and full-contact blows.

karate, jiu-jitsu, judo

FRACTURES

Hand and wrist fractures are common in karate because of the emphasis put on hand movements. Most karate movements use hand strikes, while in tae kwon do, the legs are used more often. Because of this, tae kwon do athletes sometimes suffer leg fractures. Mixed martial arts, Thai kickboxing, and Judo practitioners are at risk for fractures in the long bones and pelvis.

DISLOCATIONS

These injuries happen when a bone is suddenly moved from its normal position. Martial arts competitors are at risk for dislocations in any part of the body,

A serious wrist fracture may require surgery. Afterward, the bones will need time to heal before being used again.

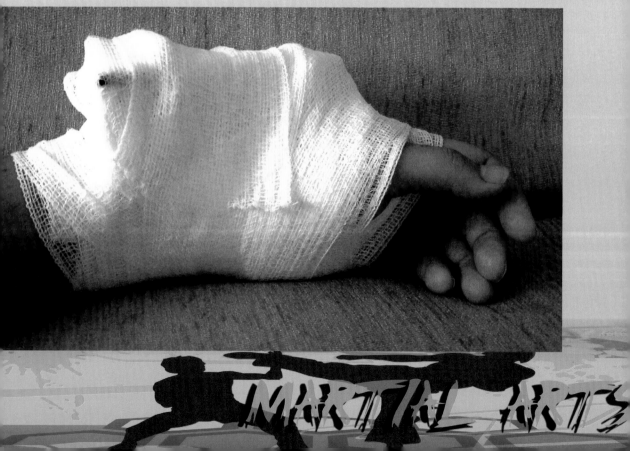

karate, jiu-jitsu, judo

but shoulders, fingers, and toes are the areas most likely to be dislocated. In jiu-jitsu and other martial arts based on wrestling, shoulder dislocations often occur. Knee dislocations are more rare in martial arts, but they can happen.

Karate-Kid finger is a common injury that happens when a student performs karate chops against partners or on boards. This almost always results from poor technique. A student will feel **acute** pain and a tingling sensation in his nerves, and his skin may look abnormal.

OVERUSE INJURY

Doing the same kick every week for years can cause an overuse injury. These injuries are no less dangerous even though they happen gradually. Karate students who feel arm pain and cannot explain why should be aware of a condition known as effort **thrombosis**, which is caused by repetitive arm movements such as punches. This condition results in blood clots in the arm that could travel to other areas of the body, causing a risk of heart attack.

The pain from overuse injury is usually more dull and subtle than the acute, sudden pain of a bone moving out of place. Make sure to consult your sensei or parent if you feel constant pain in a joint. If the pain does not stop, stop practicing and consult a doctor.

Severe Injuries

Martial arts' injuries are occasionally dangerous, even life-threatening. Adults and older teens who are competing in tournaments are the most at risk. If you think you suffer an injury that falls under this category, completely stop participating in a tournament or practice. Let your sensei or the referees know immediately.

In full-contact sparring, if the participant receives any blows to the chest region, ribs could fracture, and the student might suffer inner bleeding.

karate, jiu-jitsu, judo

Mixed Martial Arts: The Dangers

Perhaps you have seen Ultimate Fighting Championship (UFC) fights on television. Mixed martial arts (MMA) are one of the fastest growing ways of competing, but they have considerable risks. Any full-contact sport can be dangerous, but MMA are especially so. In a study of four MMA tournaments in a four-month period, analysts found that 103 episodes of neck injury occurred among 427 athletes who took part. Five of those participants were hospitalized.

Some people are calling for more regulations on MMA to prevent the brutal levels of some UFC matches. For instance, Senator John McCain is completely against UFC matches, calling them "barbaric . . . not a sport"; he even described UFC fights as "human cockfighting." (A cockfight is the practice of placing bets on roosters put in cages together to fight to the death.)

On the other hand, Joshua Landa, a surgeon in New York City, calls such statements from John McCain merely "anecdotal." (Anecdotal evidence is evidence that relies on individual cases rather than actual scientific study). He points to the

karate, jiu-jitsu, judo

lack of actual studies of mixed martial arts and states that the risk is similar to that of boxing, which everyone accepts.

While the media often portray MMA as brutal and dangerous, supporters point out that there had never been a death or crippling injury in an organized MMA event in North America until the death of Sam Vasquez on November 30, 2007. Vasquez collapsed shortly after being knocked out by Vince Libardi in the third round of an October 20, 2007, fight in Houston, Texas. Vasquez had two separate surgeries to remove blood clots from his brain, and shortly after the second operation, he suffered a major stroke and never regained consciousness.

A study by Johns Hopkins University concluded, "The overall injury rate [excluding injury to the brain] in MMA competitions is now similar to other combat sports [involving striking], including boxing. Knockout rates are lower in MMA competitions than in boxing. This suggests a reduced risk of traumatic brain injury in MMA competitions when compared to other events involving striking."

MARTIAL ARTS

karate, jiu-jitsu, judo

If you feel you are unusually out of breath after a blow to the chest, or if you feel air escaping from the chest, seek medical attention. Blows to the lower abdomen should be treated just as cautiously, since they can cause liver, spleen, and kidney injuries. Martial artists who engage in tournaments where there are throws, grabs, and grapples (gripping motions), such as jiu-jitsu and judo tournaments, are at risk for spine injury. Neck injuries from being thrown onto the mat can be as bad as the whiplash caused by a car crash. Serious spinal injuries can even result in paralysis.

karate, jiu-jitsu, judo

Breaking Boards, Not Bones.

Following good form when breaking boards or bricks could save you some painful injuries. Some studies have found a higher incident of injury for breaking boards than in sparring.

What to Do If You Are Injured

Be aware that this is not a complete list. Doctors and medics spend years studying medicine, and the medical textbook from one class is hundreds of times the length of this book. These are merely some guidelines on what to do if you are injured. Always seek professional medical help as well.

- Stop participating when you feel that you may have an injury. Trust your feelings.

- Promptly go to a doctor. By doing so immediately, you may reduce your recovery time later.

- Treat sprains, muscle sprains, or bruises with rest and an icepack. Elevate the limb above your heart.

- Do not go back to practicing your martial art until you are fully recovered. If your injury fell into the medium to severe category consult a doctor before beginning again.

To avoid injuries, good form is particularly important when breaking boards.

5
Nutrition and Supplements

Understanding the Words

A **nutritionist** is an expert in nutrition; she can help you put together a healthy diet that is right for your body's needs.

Synthesis is the process of putting something together.

If something is **fortified**, it has been made stronger (or more nutritious) than normal.

Stamina is strength and energy that keeps on going (like the Energizer® bunny!)

Something that is **anti-inflammatory** reduces pain and swelling.

karate, jiu-jitsu, judo

The martial arts student should not confine training to only the dojo. To perform martial arts well, the practitioner must also eat well. Eating healthy keeps the mind aware and the body prepared for taxing workouts. When the body trains, it breaks down and needs to rebuild muscle. Food is an important way to recover from a rigorous workout. Furthermore, good diets support the body and keep it healthy. A sick martial arts student cannot train and will not rise to higher belts as fast. A strong, healthy athlete will feel better and perform better in tournaments and the dojo.

Healthy eating does not always require eating less. In fact, the opposite is usually the case. Athletes need to fuel their bodies more than people who do not work out. When you begin to workout regularly, you will feel a greater need to eat. This is natural! Remember also—exercise helps you to lose fat, but some of your weight will now go to muscles, creating a slimmer look that may not be reflected on your scales.

> **DID YOU KNOW?**
> Bananas have a lot of simple carbohydrates, but are also filled with vitamins, minerals, and fiber. Most simple carbs should be avoided, but bananas are an exception!

The young person who is inactive needs to consume around 2,000 calories per day; women need to consume less than that, about 1,800 calories. Martial arts students, however, require more calories. Researchers have found that tae kwon do athletes need around 3,500 calories per day, and even then, they will lose a small amount of weight. Some sparring tournaments have weight classes, so losing a set amount of weight or gaining an amount of weight to be in a higher weight bracket may be important.

This difference in required diets does not mean that athletes should stock up on junk food to make up for the amount of energy they burn. What an athlete eats is as important as how much. Beyond the volume of calories, an athlete should consume the correct amount of nutrients, as well as daily vitamins and minerals.

karate, jiu-jitsu, judo

The following is a list of the major food groups that are found in a healthy diet for a martial-arts student.

Carbohydrates

Carbohydrates provide energy to the body. Between 50 and 65 percent of an athlete's diet should be carbohydrates. Think of carbohydrates (also known simply as "carbs") as the fuel you need to keep your body running through workouts and tournaments.

There are two types of carbohydrates: simple and complex. Simple carbohydrates break down faster and provide a burst of energy but then let your body down fast. Usually they are full of empty calories: food that doesn't enrich the body but has a high amount of calories. Most teenagers know and love simple carbohydrate foods—candy, soda, and other sweets—but an athlete should avoid these foods. While athletes should avoid empty-calorie foods at all times, they should especially steer clear of these foods before workouts to avoid a "crash" or feeling a lack of energy while they workout.

Complex carbohydrates break down slower in the body and provide it with more nutrients. Vegetables, fruits, brown rice, whole grain bread, beans, nuts,

Two Simple Ways to Eat Complex Carbs

- Make half of your grains whole. Check the nutrition facts on bread, pasta, and cereal. Make sure the word "whole" is in the first ingredient and avoid the word "enriched" on the back. Because complex carbohydrates are popular, labels misleadingly call foods whole-grain when they are not.
- Eat five servings of fruit per day.

MARTIAL ARTS

karate, jiu-jitsu, judo

and cereal all contain complex carbohydrates. These complex carbohydrates give the body a more sustainable boost of energy. Health professionals agree that switching from simple to complex carbohydrates is one of the smartest dietary choices you can make. Most complex carbohydrate foods are also good sources of fiber, which helps keep your digestive system healthy as well as makes the body feel more full. This, in turn, helps weight loss.

Fruit is a great source of a variety of vitamins and nutrients. Eating fruit is also a great way to eat something sweet but healthy.

karate, jiu-jitsu, judo

Protein

Proteins are important chemicals found in all living things; these chemicals are used to perform specific functions inside our body cells. Each protein is a long, folded chain-like molecule made up of "links" called amino acids. Our bodies can break down proteins into their base amino acids and use them to build new proteins that make up our muscles and bones. For this reason, it is important to eat enough protein to give the body the building blocks it needs to become stronger, especially during exercise.

Maintaining a healthy balance of proteins in the diet is one of the surest ways to gain muscle mass. Ten to 15 percent of an average person's diet should be in protein, but some athletes may want to eat slightly more than that amount. Consuming too much protein will not mean muscles will grow faster, however; the body simply gets rid of the extra protein. To know how much protein to eat, a good rule of thumb is that the number of grams should be equal to about one-third of your body weight in pounds. For example, a 200-pound person should have roughly 70 grams of protein per day.

Two types of protein are animal protein and vegetable protein. Animal protein can be found in eggs, milk and cheese. Vegetable protein can be found in wheat, rye, and green vegetables.

Fats

Although fats have a bad reputation, your body needs fat! Fats help build up the body and can be used as sources of energy. Healthy skin, teeth,

DID YOU KNOW?

Scientists created trans fats to preserve foods longer on the shelf. Many packaged foods like chips and microwavable popcorn contain trans fats. Fast-food restaurants also often put trans fats in foods such as french fries. But the health effects of eating trans fat are numerous and range from obesity and heart disease to infertility in women and Alzheimer's in older people.

karate, jiu-jitsu, judo

Cholesterol

A lot of bad things have been said about cholesterol—but most of this bad press focuses on LDLs, or low-density lipo-proteins, a kind of cholesterol that can clog our blood vessels and make our hearts work harder. Our bodies make this cho-lesterol out of saturated fats, like those found in animal fat from meats, butter, and whole milk. It is important to know, though, that there is a kind of cholesterol that has a good ef-fect on the body. HDLs, or high-density lipoproteins can be increased as easily as exercising regularly.

skin, and hair require a steady diet of fats. Also nerve functions require fats. Your body burns body fat for energy after prolonged workouts, especially ones that take more than an hour.

Fats should, however, take up no more than 25 percent of your caloric intake. The kinds of fat one consumes make a difference as well; not all fats are alike.

Fats can be classified as: polyunsaturated, monounsaturated fats, and saturated fats. Unsaturated fat is good for the body and saturated fats are best avoided. Monounsaturated fats (MUFA) such as nuts, avocados, canola, and olive-oil are all high in MUFA, and these foods can even help contribute to weight loss. Polyunsaturated fats such as salmon, fish oil, corn, and soy lower cholesterol. Omega 3 fatty acids are polyunsaturated and are found in fish oil, contributing to such benefits as healthier heart performance, cancer prevention, and mental health.

karate, jiu-jitsu, judo

On the other hand, excess fat intake has negative effects, especially if you're eating too much saturated fat. Meat, dairy, eggs, and seafood all contain saturated fats. Other oils such as coconut oil and palm oil also have this "bad fat." Eating too much of these saturated fats contributes to a sluggish feeling. Any kind of fat takes from three to five hours to fully digest, so stock up on carbohydrates for energy instead of any fatty foods.

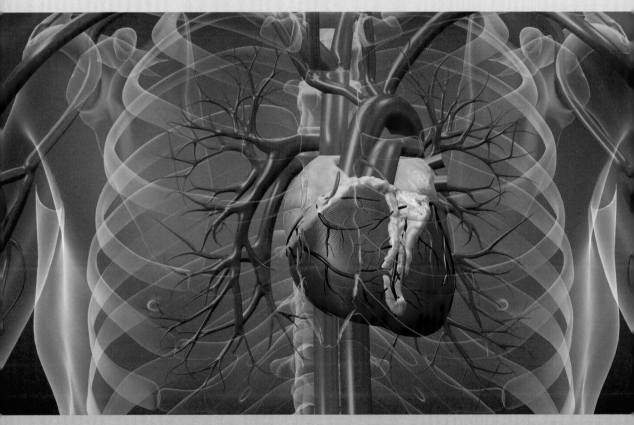

Eating excessive amounts of food high in cholesterol and fat can lead to an increased chance of heart disease and other health issues.

karate, jiu-jitsu, judo

No Shortcuts

A diet should be balanced. There are no short cuts and there is no substitute for moderation. Apply the structure and discipline of the dojo to your eating habits.

Water

Water has been called the most important of all nutrients. The body is made up of 60 percent water, and all parts of the body depend on water to function. By hydrating our bodies (filling them with water), we rejuvenate all parts of our bodies, including our brains. Water transports nutrients around the body and helps regulate temperature and metabolism. Water should be consumed before, during, and after exercise, and athletes should drink at least eight glasses of water a day.

The best diet in the world is no good if you become dehydrated. Dehydration occurs when your body doesn't have enough water, leading to fatigue, dizziness, and headaches, all of which can hurt your physical performance.

Listen to Your Body

It is important to listen to your body—and obey it. That may mean drinking when you feel thirsty during a training—or stopping eating before the end of a meal because you feel full. There is no reason to dehydrate your body or needlessly overeat. Your body sends you important signals. You just have to learn to listen.

karate, jiu-jitsu, judo

Drinking enough water before, during, and after physical activity is vitally important to maintaining health and athletic performance.

karate, jiu-jitsu, judo

It's best to carry a bottle of water with you the whole day before going to the dojo or to a tournament, to make sure you are fully hydrated. In addition, you should be drinking water throughout the training or tournament, to avoid becoming dehydrated as you sweat.

Staying fully hydrated has many benefits. Besides helping your physical performance, it can help concentration, improve digestive health, and reduce the risk of kidney stones.

Eating Healthy

So-called "health food" has become popular. In a walk down the aisles of a supermarket in America you will find many brightly decorated boxes claiming in large, gaudy letters that they will help you become healthier or thinner. Make up your own mind about what's good for you by checking out the nutrition information on each package. When it comes to health benefits, do not believe everything you see on the packaging. If every word of self-advertisement were true, we would all be living in paradise. Many packages will over-exaggerate their benefits. Be aware of what is actually in the food, rather than what it says on the outside of the box. The fewer ingredients that are in the food, the richer it will be in nutrients. Most of those huge words on the back of the health bar or cereal box are excess preservatives which will need to be burned off. Look for foods that are as close to their natural source as possible.

karate, jiu-jitsu, judo

Dietary Supplements

Many athletes seek to improve their performance by taking dietary supplements—pills or drinks that contain nutrients or chemicals—to improve their performance during a game. Dietary supplements do not include illegal performance-enhancing drugs. Instead, they contain vitamins, minerals, or chemicals that help the body use those vitamins more efficiently.

Before taking any supplements ask: do I really need this? Supplements should not be taken if they are not needed. Before you use a supplement, try to find a way to integrate that vitamin or mineral into your diet. For example, if your diet is lacking in calcium, you could drink more milk; if your diet lacks Vitamin C, then you could stock up on oranges, peppers, and broccoli.

Not all diets are complete and some vitamins are less accessible than others. For instance, most Western diets are low in seafood, so taking fish oil supplements makes up for the lack in omega 3 acids fish. Due to poor soil in the United States, even if fruits and vegetables are eaten regularly, they may not be as rich in nutrients as they should be.

When properly used, supplements can improve overall health and performance, but you should always consult a doctor or nutritionist before taking them. Some examples of common supplements include vitamin tablets, creatine, protein shakes or powder, and ginseng.

VITAMIN AND MINERAL TABLETS

We do not always get the vitamins and nutrients we need, usually because our diets are not as balanced as they should be. Sometimes, it's because the foods available to us have been processed in such a way that they lose their nutrients. Also, exhausted soil all over the country means that

DID YOU KNOW?

Your doctor can tell you if you have a vitamin or mineral deficiency by doing various tests. She can also help you examine your diet to determine if you're not eating enough of some vitamin or mineral.

MARTIAL ARTS

karate, jiu-jitsu, judo

Eating Like a Sumo Wrestler

If you don't want to be fit and want to gain body fat without gaining muscle-mass then follow these real sumo diet rules:

- Miss breakfast. Your body will burn off excess fat slower without a kick-start in the morning which breakfast provides.
- Continue not to eat while you exercise. Without food, the body will conserve fat even during exercise.
- When you must eat, take a nap immediately after. Do not ever let your body get the chance to burn off excess fat.
- Eat your last meal as late in the night as possible and eat the most in your late dinner.

Lessons from the Sumo Diet

The principle behind a sumo wrestler's eating habits is to trick the brain into storing fat by ignoring the body's needs. So do the opposite in terms of when to eat. Eat a generous breakfast and a large lunch when you're active. As early at night as you can, eat a light dinner.

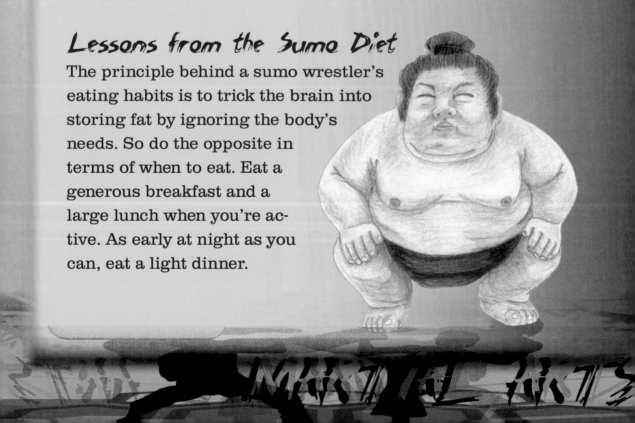

karate, jiu-jitsu, judo

fruits and vegetables are often not as nutrient-rich as they should be. In many cases, we can get vitamins we need from vitamin supplements. These supplements, usually taken as pills, contain a balanced mixture of vitamins and nutrients known as multivitamins. Sometimes they contain a single vitamin or mineral that our diet is lacking.

Be careful when taking vitamin supplements, however, because it is possible to overdose on certain ones. Don't take more than the required amount. Any excess vitamin intake will leave the body or be stored in the kidneys. It is possible to overdose on those vitamins that the body stores. Some vitamin supplements are infused with more than is required daily. For instance, B6

Taking a daily vitamin pill is a good idea, but never exceed the recommended dosage.

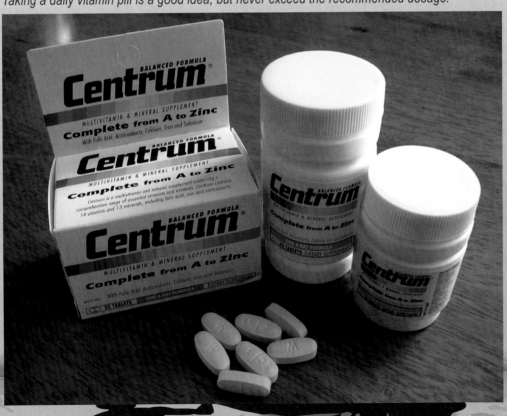

karate, jiu-jitsu, judo

vitamins are sold in one-gram quantities, but the body only needs up to two milligrams per day. Therefore, you should only take a one-gram tablet every two days, because an overdose of vitamin B6 can cause sensory and motor control loss. Other vitamins have equally harmful effects if taken in excess; Vitamin E overdoses, for instance, cause blood clots, tumors, fatigue, and reproductive problems. Vitamin A causes fatigue and dry and itchy skin.

When it comes to vitamin and mineral supplements, there is such thing as too much of a good thing. Don't assume that more is always better! And don't forget to always talk to your doctor before beginning supplements of any kind.

CREATINE

Creatine is a specific protein naturally found in your body's muscle cells. When taken in larger doses than is found in the body, creatine has the effect of increasing the rate of protein synthesis within your body's cells. You will have more energy to exercise, and you will see a greater improvement in strength and speed when you do. However, putting any chemical into your body can have negative effects, and you should talk to a doctor before starting creatine. Creatine is only suited for adult athletes, though, so young people under the age of seventeen should not take it.

PROTEIN SUPPLEMENTS

Eating protein immediately after a workout is recommended in order to refuel your body, because protein helps build and repair muscles. Getting enough protein from the food you eat, however, can be difficult. Not many people feel like preparing a meal right after exercising, so protein shakes are often a convenient and healthy choice. Many shakes contain blends of protein, carbohydrates, and fats, and some include vitamins to help balance an athlete's diet. You should always remember, however, that while protein shakes are useful for supplementing your diet, they should never be used to replace

karate, jiu-jitsu, judo

Eggs are an excellent source of protein.

meals in significant quantities. Your body still needs plenty of nutrients that it can only get from a balanced diet. No matter how **fortified** a protein shake may be, it cannot adequately replace a real meal. A nutritionist can tell you how to fit protein or supplement shakes into your diet safely and effectively.

GINSENG

Ginseng is an herb that has been used in Chinese medicine for centuries to increase awareness and energy. Today, ginseng is available in a variety of

karate, jiu-jitsu, judo

Ginseng comes from a plant with red berries. It has been used medicinally in China for hundreds of years. Do not take it, however, without talking to your doctor.

ways: in capsules, powders, in different kinds of teas, and in energy drinks. Dosages and potency vary widely.

Supporters of ginseng claim it increases muscle capacity by raising an athlete's stamina; in other words it, decreases tiredness during practice. They also claim ginseng improves mental alertness. Ginseng has uses outside of athletics, because of beneficial effects such as increased blood volume, and anti-inflammatory action. Chinese doctors also use ginseng as a cold remedy.

karate, jiu-jitsu, judo

Side effects for ginseng will depend on the different brand and are usually rare. Headaches, nausea, and insomnia may sometimes accompany the energy boost that comes from ginseng. Ginseng also can cause nervousness and anxiety, especially among first-time users. Pregnant women should avoid using it. Before taking ginseng, consult a doctor if you are taking any prescribed medications or other supplements.

Opinions vary about the use of ginseng among athletes. In studies where one group was given real ginseng and others were given pills that did nothing (called placebos), there was almost no performance difference between those who took the placebo and those who took the real ginseng.

Ultimately, there is no substitute for sleep and training, and no better way to stay mentally aware than to meditate. Probably the best way to stay fit and excel in martial arts is to avoid fatty foods (mostly the ones we already knew we shouldn't eat), bulk up, and hydrate ourselves, and above all practice at the dojo. There is absolutely no substitute on earth for consistent hard work.

6
The Dangers of Performance-Enhancing Drugs

Understanding the Words

Cerebral *has to do with your mind's thinking abilities.*

To stimulate means to encourage something to happen, to trigger a response.

Infertility *is the inability to produce sperm or eggs; someone who is infertile cannot have biological children.*

A hormone is a chemical in your body that helps control and regulate the activity of a body system (such as your reproductive system).

Insomnia *is a condition that makes it difficult to fall asleep or stay asleep.*

Hypertension *is the medical term for having high blood pressure.*

Hallucinations *are when a person sees something or someone that is not really there.*

karate, jiu-jitsu, judo

For many professional athletes, the pressure to perform well is intense. Athletes face stress from everyone around them to constantly improve their skill, strength, and speed. Sometimes, an athlete turns to chemical enhancements to reach a level of competitive performance of which he would not normally be capable. This is never legal, and is almost always dangerous, but nevertheless, some players feel compelled to use performance-enhancing drug.

What Are Drugs?

In general, a drug is anything you place into your body that changes your body's chemistry in some way. Drugs can be useful or beneficial, such as the tablets you might take when you have a headache or antibiotics developed to fight diseases. Drugs can also be very dangerous. In fact, even useful, beneficial drugs almost always have the potential to be dangerous as well.

There are two families of drugs athletes sometimes abuse: performance-enhancing drugs, which boost the body's performance in a tournament or during training, and recreational drugs, which do not claim to help athletic skills but are abused for their effects. Traditional martial arts seldom involve much abuse of either category of drugs.

No Need for Drugs: The Self-Confidence Given by Martial Arts

The feeling of pride in mastering a new technique, the inner strength discovered when the brown belt breaks through three sets of boards, the immense accomplishment of becoming a black belt, all these contribute to the healthy self-respect that comes from practicing martial arts. As a result, few practitioners of martial arts feel any need to alter either their bodies or their minds with drugs.

MARTIAL ARTS

karate, jiu-jitsu, judo

The sense of genuine confidence and mastery that comes from learning a martial art can never be produced by any drug.

MARTIAL ARTS

karate, jiu-jitsu, judo

This does not mean, of course, that no martial arts student has ever mis-used alcohol or drugs, but the majority of martial artists abstain from abusing drugs and alcohol. The need for a clear mind and the importance martial arts place on discipline wards off the temptation to abuse substances. All dojos teach against partaking in mild-confusing substances. Drug abuse just doesn't work while practicing martial arts.

Performance-enhancing drugs such as steroids are not widely used in martial arts either. The World Taekwondo Federation specifically prohibits any use of performance-enhancing drugs. Olympics officials also test tae kwon do athletes. There are few instances of athletes being barred from par-ticipating internationally because of drug use.

Mixed Martial Arts and Drug Abuse

WHY?

Mixed martial arts (MMA), however, have a higher rate of drug-abuse than traditional Eastern practices. Among the reasons for this could be MMA's emphasis on brute strength compared with the emphasis on technique in competitive martial arts like tae kwon do. MMA are practiced more in the United States, where the culture places an emphasis on physical prowess and the body's appearance. Eastern martial arts, on the other hand, are more cerebral and are built on Eastern religions that frown upon drug use, such as Zen Buddhism and Confucianism. MMA matches are more intense than traditional martial arts competitions, putting greater of stress on the athlete. Street drugs may also be used more often because there is a more lenient attitude toward the fighters than in traditional martial arts. Regardless of the reason behind the drug abuse, the growing number of suspensions at the highest level of MMA dirties the sport's reputation in the eyes of mainstream America.

karate, jiu-jitsu, judo

Because mixed martial arts require more brute strength, participants may be tempted to abuse steroids.

STEROIDS

The most common performance enhancers are anabolic steroids. These chemicals are similar to testosterone, which is the male hormone naturally produced by the body to help **stimulate** muscle growth. That's why when a player takes anabolic steroids, he receives a boost to his speed and strength that is greater than what the body could normally produce on its own. Almost every organized sport considers this cheating.

karate, jiu-jitsu, judo

Steroids can cause an unhealthy increase in cholesterol levels and an increase in blood pressure. This stresses the heart and leads to an increased risk of heart disease. Large doses of steroids can also lead to liver failure, and they have a negative effect on blood sugar levels, sometimes causing problems similar to diabetes. Steroids can also cause infertility.

If an adolescent (typically someone under the age of about seventeen) takes anabolic steroids, the risks are often much worse. Steroids stop bones from growing, which results in stunted growth. In addition, the risks to the liver and heart are much greater, since a young person's liver and heart are not fully matured and are more susceptible to the damage that steroids can

Although steroids have legal uses, the illegal market has grown, supported in large part by athletes and bodybuilders. These huge quantities of steroids were confiscated by the U.S. Drug Enforcement Agency during a drug bust.

MARTIAL ARTS

karate, jiu-jitsu, judo

Ricco Rodriguez and the Effects of Recreational Drugs

Ricco Rodriguez achieved many great things during his professional fighting career. In 1997, he was one of a small number of Americans to win the Brazilian Jiu-Jitsu World Championship. Ricco then moved to fighting in MMA matches, and in his entire MMA career, he only lost eleven matches out of fifty.

Despite having won the UFC championship, however, he was demoted to fighting in lesser MMA matches. His addiction to cocaine became public when in November 2006, just after he had won a fight, officials suspended him indefinitely due to detected cocaine and marijuana use. Ricco is among many other UFC fighters who have been caught taking drugs that do not enhance performance but create a high for them.

In 2008, Ricco participated in the VH1 reality show, **Celebrity Rehab with Dr. Drew**. Since the show, he has stated he has stayed sober.

karate, jiu-jitsu, judo

cause. Furthermore, taking steroids puts you at a greater risk of psychological problems that generally begin with aggression but often lead to much more serious issues. Considering these health risks, as well as the fact that anabolic steroids are almost universally banned from organized sports, they should not be used, except by those who have legitimate medical conditions that require their use.

ANDROSTENEDIONE

Androstenedione is a hormone produced naturally by the adrenal glands, ovaries, and testes, which is then converted to testosterone and estadiol, the human sex hormones. Artificially produced androstenedione is a controlled

Miyamoto Musashi was one of Japan's greatest warriors. He is shown here doing battle with a whale.

karate, jiu-jitsu, judo

Wise Words: Miyamoto Musashi

Miyamoto Musashi was one of the greatest Japanese swordsmen in the world. He fought his first duel at the age of thirteen and went on to win countless swordfights. At an old age, while suffering from what we now believe was a form of cancer, he went into a cave to live as a hermit and write a book of strategy. His **Book of Five Rings** has become a classic in military strategy and philosophy. In this book Musashi states, "Do nothing which is of no use." This quote applies to many activities martial artists should avoid doing. Eating junk food and abusing drugs are both activities that have "no use" for a martial artist.

substance that is illegal in competition in the United States, though it is still being sold.

Scientific evidence suggests that androstenodione doesn't promote muscle growth, and it has several serious risks. In men, side effects include acne, diminished sperm production, shrunken testicles, and enlargement of breasts. In women, the drug causes acne and masculinization, such as growth of facial hair. Androstenedione has also been shown to increase the chances of a heart attack and stroke because it causes the buildup of bad cholesterol.

karate, jiu-jitsu, judo

STIMULANTS

Stimulants are a class of drugs that increase breathing rate, heart rate, and blood circulation. Athletes believe these drugs stimulate their central nervous system, allowing them to perform better. Stimulants such as caffeine, cold remedies, and street drugs (cocaine and methamphetamine) can promote alertness, suppress appetite, and increase aggressiveness. However, these drugs can also make an athlete have difficulty concentrating, as well as insomnia, nervousness, and irritability. Athletes can even become psychologically addicted. Other side effects include weight loss, tremors, heart rate abnormalities, hypertension, hallucinations, and heart attacks.

OVER-THE-COUNTER DRUGS

Besides these dangerous and often illegal drugs, athletes also use painkillers and sedatives to enhance their performance. Painkillers allow athletes to operate with a higher level of pain tolerance, while sedatives allow them to concentrate under stressful situations. However, these drugs can also decrease performance.

THE CONSEQUENCES OF PERFORMANCE-ENHANCING DRUG USE

MMA competitors, like all athletes, are often looking for a greater competitive edge to gain fame, acclaim, or an award or prize. However, there is no magical concoction that will automatically bring these rewards. Instead, these performance-enhancing drugs have many adverse side effects that could harm the body and its performance more than they help.

MARTIAL ARTS

karate, jiu-jitsu, judo

Further Reading

Bare Grounds, Trish. *The Bare Essentials Guide for Martial Arts Injury Prevention and Care.* Wethersfield, Conn.: Turtle Press, 2001.

Braun, Christian. *Fitness for Fighters.* Aachen, Germany: Meyer & Meyer Fachverlag und Buchhandel GmbH, 2009.

Cochran, Sean. *Complete Conditioning for Martial Arts.* Champaign, Ill.: Human Kinetics, 2001.

Lawler, Jennifer and Laura Kamienski. *Training Women in the Martial Arts: A Special Journey.* Terre Haute, Ind.: Wish Publishing, 2007.

Penn, B.J, Glen Cordoza, and Erich Krauss. *Mixed Martial Arts: The Book of Knowledge.* Las Vegas: Victory Belt Publishing, 2007.

Price, Robert G. *Ultimate Guide to Weight Training for Martial Arts.* Cleveland, Ohio: Sportsworkout.com, 2007.

Sprague, Martina. *Strength and Power Training for Martial Arts.* Wethersfield, Conn.: Turtle Press, 2005.

karate, jiu-jitsu, judo

Find Out More on the Internet

Complete Martial Arts
www.completemartialarts.com

Martial Arts Network
martial-arts-network.com

Martial Arts.org
www.martialarts.org

Sports Injury Bulletin—Martial Arts Injury Overview
www.sportsinjurybulletin.com/archive/martial-arts.html

USA Dojo
www.usadojo.com/youth-center/youth-center.htm

World Martial Arts Information Center
www.martialinfo.com

Disclaimer

The websites listed on this page were active at the time of publication. The publisher is not responsible for websites that have changed their address or discontinued operation since the date of publication. The publisher will review and update the websites upon each reprint.

Bibliography

Birrer, R.B., MD MPH, FACEP, FACSM and S.P. Halbrook, PhD. "Martial Arts Injuries: The Results of a Five Year National Survey." *The American Journal of Sports Medicine*, July 1988, 16 (4): 408–410.

Borkowski, Cezar and Marion Manzo. *The Complete Idiot's Guide to Martial Arts.* New York, NY: Alpha Books, 1999.

The Canyon. "Bigger Faster, Higher—MMA Fighters Busted for Drug Abuse," www.thecyn.com/blog/bigger-faster-higher-mma-fighters-busted-for-drug-abuse (10 March 2010).

Cochran, Sean. *Complete Conditioning for Martial Arts.* Champaign, Ill.: Human Kinetics, 2001.

Concrete Jungle Self-Defense. "Statistics (don't be one!)," www.cjselfdefense.com/statistics.shtml (17 March 2010).

Diet Blog. "Sumo Wrestlers: This is How You Get Fat," www.diet-blog.com/archives/2005/03/21/sumo_wrestlers_this_is_how_you_get_fat.php (10 March 2010).

Eden, Karen. *The Complete Idiot's Guide to Tae Kwon Do*. New York, NY: Alpha Books, 1999.

eHow. "How to Become a Professional MMA Fighter," www.ehow.com/how_2037532_professional-mma-fighter.html (18 March 2010).

karate, jiu-jitsu, judo

Gibson, Adam and Bill Wallace. *Competitive Karate: Featuring the Super-foot System*. Champaign, Ill.: Human Kinetics, 2004.

Go for your Life. "Martial Arts—Preventing Injury," www.goforyourlife.vic.gov.au/hav/articles.nsf/pages/Martial_arts_preventing_injury?open (15 March 2010).

Hassell, Randall G. "Stiff Mind, Stiff Body." *Black Belt*, December 1985.

Kim, Sang H. "Nutrition for Martial Artists," www.martialarts-101.com/martial_arts_nutrition.asp (15 March 2010).

Landa, Joshua, MD. "Risk and Injuries in Contact Fighting," *Journal of Combative Sport*, Aug 2004, ejmas.com/jcs/2004jcs/jcsart_landa_0804.htm (17 March 2010).

Lopez, Miguel. "Gracie Tests Positive for Drug," www.martialartsgazette.com (11 March 2010).

Man Lee, Soon and Gaetane Ricke. "Official Taekwondo Training Manual," books.google.com/books?id=6yfekcezCZ8C&pg=PA265&dq=doping+AND+tae+kwon+do&client=firefox-a&cd=2#v=onepage&q=&f=false (11 March 2010).

Martial Arts of the World. "The Martial Arts List," www.maotw.com/list/ma01.html (18 March 2010).

MMA Weekly. "Drug Use in Mixed Martial Arts," www.mmaweekly.com/absolutenm/templates/dailynews.asp?articleid=4118&zoneid=1 (11 March 2010).

MyJobSearch. "Martial Arts Instructor," www.myjobsearch.com/careers/martial-arts-instructor.html (18 March 2010).

Nishiyama, Hidetaka and Richard C. Brown. *Karate the Art of "Empty-Hand" Fighting*. Boston, Mass.: Tuttle Publishing, 2000.

Pawlett, Mark and Ray Pawlett. *The Tae Kwon Do Handbook*. New York, NY: Rosen Publishing Group, 2008.

Sacred Texts. "Samayapalana Parva—Section XIII," www.sacred-texts.com/hin/m04/m04013.htm (17 March 2010).

Scandiffio, Laura and Nicolas Debon. *The Martial Arts Book*. Toronto, Ont.: Annick Press, 2003.

Shea, Thomas B. *Paper Wraps Rock: The Gentle Side of Karate*. W. Conshohocken, Penn.: Infinity Publishing, 2005.

Sports Injury Bulletin. "Martial Arts Injury Overview," www.sportsinjurybulletin.com/archive/martial-arts.html (15 March 2010).

karate, jiu-jitsu, judo

Index

karate, jiu-jitsu, judo

Picture Credits

Cerebellum; Creative Commons: p. 81
Creative Commons: pp. 58, 73
Flora Farm; Katharina Lohrie; Creative Commons: p. 76
Holistic Care; Creative Commons: p. 39
Janothird; Creative Commons: p. 54
Mabel, Joe: Creative Commons: p. 41
Stockxchng: p. 75
U.S. Army: p. 83
U.S. Drug Enforcement Administration: p. 84

To the best knowledge of the publisher, all images not specifically credited are in the public domain. If any image has been inadvertently uncredited, please notify Harding House Publishing Service, 220 Front Street, Vestal, New York 13850, so that credit can be given in future printings.

karate, jiu-jitsu, judo

About the Author and the Consultants

J. S. McIntosh is a writer living in upstate New York. He graduated from Binghamton University with a degree in English literature. He enjoys making music on his laptop, playing poker, and being a literacy volunteer. Currently, he writes on topics ranging from military history to health and fitness.

Susan Saliba, Ph.D., is a senior associate athletic trainer and a clinical instructor at the University of Virginia in Charlottesville, Virginia. A certified athletic trainer and licensed physical therapist, Dr. Saliba provides sports medicine care, including prevention, treatment, and rehabilitation for the varsity athletes at the university. Dr. Saliba is a member of the national Athletic Trainers' Association Educational Executive Committee and its Clinical Education Committee.

Eric Small, M.D., a Harvard-trained sports medicine physician, is a nationally recognized expert in the field of sports injuries, nutritional supplements, and weight management programs. He is author of *Kids & Sports* (2002) and is Assistant Clinical professor of pediatrics, Orthopedics, and Rehabilitation Medicine at Mount Sinai School of Medicine in New York. He is also Director of the Sports Medicine Center for Young Athletes at Blythedale Children's Hospital in Valhalla, New York. Dr. Small has served on the American Academy of Pediatrics Committee on Sports Medicine, where he develops national policy regarding children's medical issues and sports.